Abused but Not Forsaken

Paula Biancalana

Abused but Not Forsaken
Copyright © 2019 by Paula Biancalana
All rights reserved. No part of this book may be reproduced or transmitted in any form or by any means without written permission of the author.

ISBN 978-1-662-90028-0

Library of Congress Control Number: 2020941725

To learn more about the author please visit
www.abusedbutnotforsaken.com

This book was written in loving memory of Jane.

Table of Contents

My Family 1
My Early Years 13
Ten Years Old 25
My Teen Years 37
My Early Twenties 55
Deceived by the Enemy 67
Moving Forward 75
My Revelation 91
A New Life 101
Generational Curses 107
Recommended Reading 117

Chapter One
My Family

I grew up in a dysfunctional family, just like so many others have. I am not saying that every moment of my life was horrible, but when it was bad, it was really bad. I was born to Henry and Jane, both of whom are now deceased. I was smack dab in the middle of six children. Please know I am not here to exploit or hurt anyone—that's not my intention. I want to tell my story so that people's lives might be transformed. It is my prayer that you can get free from the chains of abuse. Feelings don't just go away—the trauma; hurt, pain, and wounds are deeply imbedded in our souls. Please know that this is my personal story about me, my life, and what I experienced.

My Family

I want to help others who are suffering from these generational iniquities that are operating in families through their bloodlines. Please know that when you or someone in your bloodline sinned and never repented this horrible cycle could have begun. It does not stop until we accept Jesus Christ as our Lord and Savior and receive salvation. Yes, we are a new creation in Christ and our sins are forgiven. But, we have these huge wounds in our soul that will play out in our lives. Please know that wounds in your soul open you up to ongoing spiritual attacks and as a result of this, they have a legal right to be there. So ultimately, you will stay depressed, sad, physically ill, and broken. I want you to know the truth and how to get free from the chains that abuse leaves victims in, sometimes for decades. It's taken me years to get free and I am still going through the healing process.

My Family

I want to tell you that there is hope and it is only found in Jesus Christ and what He did for us at Calvary, but, you have to do some of the work. Jesus is the antidote for every problem that you have in your life. It's through the blood that He shed that we are given the power to break the chains that are holding us back from living the life that He died to give us. He is the chain breaker! Please do not make the mistake of doing nothing. Begin your healing process today. Don't wait another minute; ask Jesus into your heart today and your life will never be the same.

I knew from a very young age that something was not right. I lived in an environment of fear and hostility. I wasn't a happy child and I had many emotional outbursts because I was emotionally disturbed. I was often sickly and plagued with illness. I can remember being in the hospital on three separate occasions for pneumonia. I was depressed and sad. I was holding on to some deep, dark secrets about my family life. I was a very sensitive child. Meaning I was empathic and felt things more than the average person does. That's just the way I was wired.

Both of my parents were born into very dysfunctional homes where they both endured abuse, fear, rejection, poverty, misfortune, loss, and oppression. Both were uneducated, making it more difficult to break the cycle. My mother once told me that their family was on government assistance and there was a picture in the local newspaper with a caption asking others to help their family.

My parents were born during the Depression era and it wasn't a good time for families. Did you know that during a famine or challenging time's people will do things that will affect their lives for generations? It's quite evident to see this in the Israelites eleven-day journey. You see, many of us have ancestors that made bad choices and they have been passed down to us. Unfortunately, we could be affected by these things and not even know why. I didn't know why things were happening to me.

My mother came from a home of fifteen children. There were nine girls and six boys, and her father, my grandfather, was a harsh and controlling man that would not let them go to school. My mother and her siblings were forced to work in his food factory all day long. Because of my mother's rigid upbringing and the depressing environment that she had to endure, she ran away from home at the age of eighteen.

My grandmother gave birth to sixteen children but one died after childbirth. I can't even fathom anyone having sixteen children. How did they feed all those children during the depression? I often wonder if it was my grandmother's choice to have so many children. My grandparents are both deceased now, but what I can remember about my grandmother was that it seemed she was a very passive person. I never heard my grandmother speak; she nodded and just went along with things and didn't say a word. I often wondered why. Was she afraid to talk?

In 1952 my father was twenty-six years old and he was returning home from the Korean War. At that time, my mother was nineteen years old and was living in an apartment above a grocery store. I had heard that she had no money and was getting food from the store below her. One day, my mother happened to be in the grocery store when my father was there. So this beautiful young lady who was lost, hurting, and hungry was just looking for someone to love her. On that day, she met my father. This event would change both of their lives for a very long time. Sadly, I often heard my father say, "I wish I never went to that grocery store on that day!" But I wonder if my mother wished that same thing.

My mother ran away from her horrible life situation with her parents and she ended up leaping into another horrible situation with my father. It was like a magnet pulling her into the same cycle. Little did she know that my father was her father with a different face?

Do you see how the abuse cycle sets people up? It's not until we gain a sense of awareness that we can see the path and the red flags life is sending, and all of the cycles and patterns that abuse keeps you in. It's is not your fault!

My father was Mexican American; he was born in Bay Town, Texas in 1926. My father told me much later on in my adult life that he endured many injustices as a child. He was often left with different families while his father was away looking for work. That's what his father told him. But his father was married six times during his lifetime. Because my father was left with different families he was subjected to harsh, cruel people and circumstances. His mother and father were no longer together because of some strange circumstances that I don't know all the facts on.

    I had heard once from a family member that my father's mother was caught speaking to another man in town at a market. In those days, if you were caught doing something like this you were driven out of town, and that is what happened to my grandmother. She was driven out of the small town where they lived. This was a horrible situation for my father and his two brothers to be in. They were left under the supervision of people that they did not know.

I don't know what happened to his siblings, but I am sure they endured difficult things too. My father told me that he was forced to live in a tool shed as a five-year old. He was not allowed to go into the house of the people he was staying with. So that dirty old tool shed is where he lived and slept at night. He was forced to live in darkness as a child. My father told me later that he often urinated on himself because he was so full of fear. He said that he ate things that he did not want to just to survive.

Like me, my father did not have a good beginning. But I had no knowledge of this until I got older and began to have a relationship with my father. All of his hardships were revealed much later in my life. I want to clarify that because I want you to know that these things just keep getting passed down from one generation to the next. It's the trauma in the family from our ancestors that gets passed down to the children.

My mother was Greek. She was born in Chicago in 1933. When her family got wind of the fact that she was with someone from a different nationality, her father and mother disowned her. Her father would never forgive her or speak to her again, despite the several attempts she made over the years, and he would later die. My mother was greatly distressed by this family situation and it would consume her for the rest of her life.

A root of bitterness was sown in her life which was passed down to me. She never had the chance to straighten things out with her father and I believe that she always regretted that. It was never mentioned in our family, but my mother was on medication. I would often see little green pills in her drawers, and I believe she was depressed. My mother was a very sensitive person and so these things greatly affected her on a daily basis. I would often see her crying. As a child I did not understand what was going on. I just thought that it was the fact that my father was so cruel to her. My mother made the wrong decisions for her life and she was paying dearly for it. Like I said, she went from one horrible mess to another. My siblings and I were all paying for it!

That's just how it went in those days. You stayed with your own tribe and didn't venture out of it. My father got my mother pregnant every year until she was loaded down with six babies. All I remember from a very early age was that my father was a cruel and angry man and he liked to scream a lot. This frightened me as a child and I felt fear all the time. Although he was a very hard-working man and tried his best to provide for our family, the problems seemed to escalate when he

My Family

got home after work. Then all we heard was him accusing my mother and screaming about something.

Chapter Two
My Early Years

At the age of five years old, I was a very rebellious child. I often found myself getting into mischief at home and school. I spent most of my days in kindergarten under the teacher's desk as a punishment. My little mind was so preoccupied with worry and fear it was hard for me to focus on school. I had very hard time learning and this would follow me throughout my school life. I believe I developed a learning disability because of the emotional trauma. My parents didn't have a clue what was wrong with me. I believe I was angry about my situation and didn't know how to express my pain so I began taking things that did not belong to me. I found myself stealing all the time. Stealing was a way for me to comfort myself. My parents couldn't afford to give me things, so I took them. I think I wasn't getting the attention that I needed. I remember one time when my sister and I were invited to a birthday party. At the party I stole a very expensive gift. They were some gold coins that were given to the birthday girl. I remember being questioned over and over, but I didn't give them back. I lied and said I didn't take them. It wasn't until a few days later that my sister saw me with the coins. She ran to my mother and told her. My mother went back to the family and returned the coins.

I was emotionally unstable because I wasn't getting what I needed from my parents. Their love and support simply was not there. My mother was depleted by caring for children and my father's ongoing fits of rage. Trying to keep him happy consumed all of her time, energy, and happiness. There was nothing left over to give to me or my siblings. My mother was a very kind, compassionate, and loving person and tried her best to take good care of all of us. She taught us how to be responsible and help around the house. She was an amazing cook and a wonderful housekeeper. My mother loved all of her children dearly.

My mother also loved her own family, but the division and stress of not being able to see her parents and siblings made it hard for her to enjoy life. My father hated my mother's family and they hated him too. My father often mentioned in that we were not allowed to visit her family because we were not accepted in their house because we were Mexican. Thanks to my father's rage and hatred I was never given a chance to really meet my mother's side of the family as a young child. I grew up being ashamed of my Mexican heritage, which affected my life for a very long time. I was ashamed to tell people that I was Mexican.

My father's uncontrollable temper caused so much chaos throughout my childhood. We couldn't go out to restaurants because if the waitress didn't acknowledge my father within minutes he would cause a scene in the place and begin screaming and yelling at everyone and in a fit of rage he would drag us all out. We would be scared, shaken, and embarrassed. I believe this stemmed from a root of rejection that was a stronghold in my father's life. He wasn't accepted and he experienced much prejudice in his life. He lashed out because of this deep wound in his soul. So this root of rejection was then passed onto me.

I have a particularly awful memory of sitting in the backseat of my father's car while he was driving at a fast speed swerving and trying to get around someone in front of him that was not going fast enough in my father's opinion. My father began swearing, ranting, and honking. The driver of the car in front of us stopped his car in the middle of the street and got out. My father did the same, screaming and hollering in a fit of rage. But the other driver quickly swung his fist and knocked my father out. The driver had been wearing a nice set of brass knuckles. My father was left bleeding in the middle of the street and I was terrified.

It seemed that he was always looking for trouble or something to be angry about and he carried on this way everywhere he went. He was a ticking time bomb. My father had a very loud voice so it scared me to death just to listen to him speak. He seemed to always be shouting. Once, my father bought me a radio, which I adored because I absolutely loved music. I liked to play it while I went to sleep because it was the only thing that brought me happiness. One day he got angry with me and took the radio and threw it across the room, causing it to shatter into a thousand pieces. These were just the beginning stages of what would later become emotional, physical, and verbal abuse that I would endure throughout my young life.

My father hated Christmas and birthdays, most likely because he never enjoyed them as a child. He hated to see people happy. My mother tried to have something special for us anyway—a tree and some presents—but my father wanted nothing to do with it. I never had a birthday party. *I was never celebrated as a child.* It's hard for me even now to celebrate my birthday. I was never shown that I was special or someone of value. I grew up believing this lie all my life. I have often hid in the background or the shadow so no one would notice me.

Early on, my father worked factory jobs to support us. I think he was a cab driver at one point. One day I saw my father sitting on the kitchen floor. We didn't have any chairs to sit on, just a kitchen table. He looked distraught. I look back now and realize he was probably out of a job and was wondering how he was going to make ends meet. At that time, there were five of us and my mother was pregnant with their sixth child. This particular place where we lived was plagued with constant problems. We didn't get along with our next-door neighbors. My father thought that my mother was fooling around with the guy downstairs, so every day he would harass her when he got home about how she was sleeping with the guy in the basement. I remember when I was a small child; my father repeatedly kicked my mother out of the house. She had no money and no place to go. I think she would walk the streets all day. She would come to my bedroom window at night and knock. All I could do was cry. I often wondered why my father was doing this to my mother. He would eventually let her back in. This was a constant pattern in my childhood.

Now that I am adult and have consulted people in my family about the story that was shared I have a better understanding. My father's mother was caught speaking to a man in the town and she was then sent away. This was most likely spoken about as my father grew up and this was sown as a negative seed in his heart. He probably thought that all women must be like that. This deception is what drove him to anger each day. He most likely thought about it every day. He projected this hurt and pain upon my mother and us. It was a deep wound in his soul and it operated in his life daily. He basically abused everyone in his life, even the men he worked with.

My father would tell me that I needed to speak only English because if people knew I was Mexican I would not be accepted. I grew up not even liking the fact that I was Hispanic. I was ashamed of whom I was and I didn't like myself. I hid it for most of my life. My father taught me how to hate who I was, and I often wondered why I was even born. I hated me and I didn't know what I was going to do about it. This led me on a path of self-destruction. I felt that my own parents didn't care or love me, so why should I love myself? These emotional traumas caused some deep wounds in my soul and that gave the enemy legal right to enter my life and cause havoc for me.

Later my father began a painting business with his brother. Their business began doing very well and we were able to get out of poverty. We would now be able to move away from that awful place. I asked my father later how he began this business. He stated that he saw a man who took the back seats out of his car to store things, put a few ladders on top of the vehicle, and that was it. My father told himself, if that guy could do it, so could he. One thing that I can say is that my father was a very hard worker. I had heard from my dad's employees that my father would ridicule them all day long about their work and they were scared to death of him. But, because they needed a job and money to take care of their families they took the abuse every day.

    My youngest brother was the victim of a lot of beatings, and he had to witness my mother being beaten on a frequent basis. We were all older then, but I am sure those horrible pictures stayed in his little mind and created deep wounds in his soul. He learned everything from my father's behavior. He is currently serving a life sentence in prison. I am only revealing this because if we don't put a stop to these tragedies, they just keep on getting passed down through generations. If domestic violence was recognized and exposed back then I think my mother might be alive today and my brother would have taken a different road. Unfortunately, people didn't talk about things that were going on in their families and homes. In my father's case, as in countless others, it's a soul problem. The root cause is bitterness, rejection and unforgiveness. That's why my father wouldn't let my mother work or educate herself. It was to control her so she wouldn't leave him. It's all fear based and it's a vicious cycle.

Chapter Three

Ten Years Old

My father bought a four-bedroom house on the North side of Chicago. It needed a lot of restoration. The electrical and plumbing needed to be updated. Through my father's new business, he met people that were plumbers and electricians that he would eventually hire to do the work. It was nestled in a nice neighborhood. I could walk to school every day.

Things were getting better for our family financially. With the success of his business, my father acquired more wealth and he began to change. He started buying things like rental properties. Even though my father was uneducated, he was very smart in business. He began working with one of his female clients who sold real estate and they eventually formed a partnership together. During their partnership they began having an affair. I had heard later that they had their own apartment where they would meet. My father still came home every evening and accused my mother, who was tied down with six kids, of cheating on him but he was the one doing it all the time. My mother had to endure a lot of abuse and mistreatment from my father. One day I saw my mother doing the laundry and while she was checking my father's clothing, she saw lipstick marks on his shirts. She asked him about it but he vehemently denied anything was going on.

My mother was very hurt and depressed about this situation but she had nowhere to go and no support system. She was stuck. There were no groups or counseling back then. People didn't talk about their problems. They just hid them under the rug. My mother didn't deserve such miserable treatment. She tried several times to reach out to her family, and at one point, she was able to get in contact with one of her sisters. They were able to communicate and my aunt would come to our house on special occasions, such as Easter. Easter is a huge celebration in the Greek culture.

My mother began to go to the Greek Church once in a while when my dad was not around. She would take the bus there. I remember attending services with her. I didn't understand it, but I knew that my mother was happy when she was there. She told me how when she was a child that she would go downstairs to their classroom and learn the Greek language. My mother missed her family and her culture.

After my mother's father passed, she was able to bring us kids to our grandmother's house for special occasions when my father was away.

When my father found out he was enraged with anger because he didn't want her sharing details of what was going on at our house. My mother never learned how to drive so we would all squeeze into a cab to get there. She had a very large family, but no one really talked or said anything about their personal lives. I do remember them stating their opinions that my father was a very bad man. We often sat at the table in silence and ate. My mother's family tended to sweep everything under the rug.

My mom's sister had a disabled son who lived with my grandmother, which majorly impacted my life. I have worked in the social services field for about twenty years advocating for individuals with disabilities. My cousin had nowhere to go and would stand at the door all day waiting, rocking, and smiling. As a child I often wondered who he was waiting for.

My mother also had a younger sister who was a lesbian. One of my aunts would have two sons that were homosexuals. I am just revealing this because these things are passed down in families. They are generational. But, God has given us the power to overcome these things and live in freedom. Then we can each fulfill our own purpose and destiny. We must a stand and take back our lives. Get the healing and deliverance that God has provided for us through Jesus. Let us take back everything that the enemy has stolen from us.

It was so nice to finally engage and spend time with the other part of my family. I learned that food was a big thing in my mother's family and let me tell you, my grandmother and her sisters were excellent cooks—and they cooked from scratch! I grew to love Greek food and the culture. As I got older I would just tell people that

Ten Years Old

I was Greek. I felt ashamed of my Mexican heritage and I didn't want anything to do with my father's culture so I hid it. I just wanted to shut all of that part of me out of my life!

I can remember attending a small Baptist church in Chicago. It was built in 1866 and was originally a Swedish congregation. It was a place where my brothers and sisters were happy. My brothers, sisters, and I were dropped off every Sunday by my father. I think this was a way for him to get rid of us so he could go and enjoy his secret life. But what he didn't know was that God was planting seeds in my life. God had His hand on me and I am thankful that He never let me go. I accepted Christ at the age of ten during vacation Bible school. I didn't have a clue what I was doing, but I knew that I liked church. I do believe that I would be dead right now if I had not chosen to follow Christ.

Ten Years Old

This particular Baptist church had a summer camp and my siblings and I would spend summers at the camp in Hickory Hills, Illinois. It lasted for about a week. My mother would save her money all year long for all of us to be able to go. It was good to get away even if it was only a week.

I got involved with the church choir during the week, and it was a wonderful escape for me until I got in trouble at church. I became involved with the pastor's son. We liked each other a great deal. Nothing inappropriate happened, but there were a lot of rumors. I was asked by the pastor not to return, so I didn't go back and that was the end of my church life for many years.

I received a severe beating from my father for that incident. I was told by my father quite often that I was worthless and I would never amount to anything. My father cursed me.

Specifically, he would say hurtful things like, "Get out of my sight! I am sick of you and can't wait for you to get the hell out of my life." This is what I heard from a very early age. This horrible foundation of rejection, shame, and low self-worth had been rooted in my soul. I went through life hearing these words in my mind and I felt doomed. All I wanted was to be loved. What did I do to deserve such treatment? Was it my fault?

As if the verbal abuse wasn't torment enough, the beatings began. It could be anything that would set my father off so I never knew when to expect them. I often saw my mother verbally abused or physically beaten. There wasn't a day that went by that my father wouldn't accuse my mother of cheating on him.

I lived in constant fear of what was going to happen next. I was a nervous wreck all the time. I walked on egg shells and was consumed with fear.

Ten Years Old

My brothers and sisters and I would sometimes be sitting at the kitchen table eating a meal and we would see my father coming from the garage. We would all jump up from the table in fear and run and hide in a safe place to avoid being in my father's way.

I walked with this terrible sense of dread on a daily basis, and each day only got worse. As I got older things seemed to escalate. If one of us got into trouble, we all got in trouble. My father would position us in a line for our beatings. One by one we watched in terror as the other got beat with my father's belt. I had welts all over my body. It seemed that once my father got started he couldn't control his anger and kept going until we were all screaming for our lives. All we could say while we were getting beat was, "We're sorry!" over and over again. It was just like corporal punishment.

Ten Years Old

Meal time was frightening, if I didn't finish everything on my plate I had to sit at the table until I did, no matter how long it took. I can remember sitting at the table for hours not being able to finish my tuna and peas. I hated it.

I began to see spirits in the house. They would come to my bedside and frighten me. I was the only one in my family that saw them. I can remember one night I was asleep and suddenly awakened by two spirits with turbans on their heads. They stood at the foot of my bed and stared at me. In fear I pulled the blanket over my head and cried out for my mother. Then they vanished. I have never forgotten about these things because they tormented me. I found out later that my father had gotten mixed up with the occult.

I became quite rebellious as I got older because I just didn't care anymore. I wanted to run away and do exactly what my mother did as a young woman! Do you see how these patterns and cycles keep going? How do we stop the madness from ruining our lives? These things are embedded in our minds and the trauma is deeply rooted in our souls and passed down from one generation to the next. Remember, the enemy wants to destroy you and your family!

Chapter Four
My Teen Years

When I got into high school, I was pretty quiet and passive. I was told by one of my friends that I was a doormat. I soon found out they were not my friend. But I found a group of people that accepted me and I could hang out with every day. They were hippies, with long hair and carefree attitudes. That's how I got introduced to drugs. One of my girlfriends from the group was very open about sex and drugs. I really wasn't interested, I was actually afraid at first. But because I didn't know any better and I was easily coerced into things, I tried them. First, I began using small quantities of marijuana, which I personally didn't like, but I smoked anyway. Then I was introduced to methamphetamines, which is a stimulating drug that triggers the brain's reward center. That was my drug of choice because it made me feel good and all I wanted was to feel good. I was no longer sad, it made me forget my troubles, and I had energy. I began using them every day. A student we called Slim, who sat behind me in one of my classes, sold them to me. My parents didn't take notice or even realize that I was drugged out all the time. I would stay up in my room and just listen to music for hours. Taking drugs was my way of escaping from my home life. It made me happy and I didn't feel depressed anymore. Plus, it kept me slim and trim. I was in another world all the time and I opened myself up to the dark side.

It became easier to deal with my life, although things didn't change at home. I was just able to deal with it better because I was stoned out most of my teenage years. I don't know how I even got through high school because my grades were so low. I think I got a D's and F's in every course and I am sure I made it out of there by the skin of my teeth.

I had begun sneaking out of the house at night to see my boyfriend. After a few times, I got caught and my father warned me about the consequences. He warned me several times, but I didn't care what he said. In my mind, he had ruined my life. So I continued to sneak out and eventually my father kicked me out of the house. I had to find a place to live with no money and no real place to go. I was fifteen years old and in my second year of high school. Later, one of my older girl friends would hear about my situation. She lived with her boyfriend in a coach house. He was the drummer of a rock band. She was so nice to me and told me that I could stay upstairs in their attic. I really didn't know what else to do so I accepted her offer to stay with them. Her boyfriend did not want me there and made sure that I knew it. He often fought with her about it, and he was very jealous that I was taking her time away from him. I was frightened of him so I hid in the attic and stayed there most of the time until friends would come and visit me.

For the next two years I lived away from home with my friend. This experience exposed me to a lot of older individuals and drugs like cocaine. Because my friend's boyfriend was a band member, he had many friends that would come to the house. I still managed to go to school and do the best I could. It was a very hard and dark time for me.

I had a boyfriend in high school until my senior year. He was older than me and was a nice guy. But because I was emotionally unstable, he soon ditched me for someone else. When I think back now, I believe I really cared for him. But I didn't really know what that meant at the time. I just remember having a lot of temper tantrums and being out of control. We fought a lot because I needed attention. Plus, violence was all I knew and saw in my home. He once told me that I was crazy and out of control, and, truthfully, he was right. At one point I even cut all my hair. I had long, beautiful hair but in my senior year I cut my hair very short, which made people in my school talk about me. I think they thought I was a lesbian. But, I did it for attention.

After graduation, I knew I wanted to do something with my life so I enrolled in beauty school. Later I would receive grant money to pay for my tuition, and I was also able to get a job as a waitress. In beauty school I had really tough time learning plus I had extremely low self-esteem. It took me longer than others to learn things, although I enjoyed learning to cut hair and eventually got very good at it. I managed to stay in the field for a long time. But in school I couldn't pass the tests. I took them over and over. I just couldn't pass the test to get my license. But, later on down the road, I was able to retake the test again and I finally passed.

While I was in Beauty College I met some friends that were lesbians and I began to hang out with them. The family of one of my friends from high school owned a restaurant and bar so I worked there for a while to earn money to live. Over time, I would end up staying in one of the rooms upstairs above the restaurant. This is when I began to drink, which was very destructive. I fell in love with alcohol. I started drinking while I was working at the bar. But I was wounded emotionally and alcohol became my friend, even though it brought out the worst in me. When I got drunk I got very angry and the people around could not handle me so they left me all alone. I began going to gay bars with my new friends. I wasn't twenty-one but I was able to sneak into clubs.

In the cosmetology field, a lot of the hairdressers used cocaine while they were working. This soon became my new drug of choice. Plus, I was still a bad alcoholic. I don't even know how I got home sometimes. I would often find myself the next day with no money, no purse, and in the house of someone that I didn't even know. I am lucky to be alive! Someone was watching over me.

Every person that I got involved with was an alcoholic, drug addict, or dealer. All of my boyfriends throughout those years were drug dealers and the risk of violence came with dating them. I put myself in some dangerous situations. I believe it's because I had no hope and I didn't care if I lived or died. I was barely surviving. The drugs became more frequent and stronger. I began doing Heroin and then smoking crack cocaine. I met a dealer one weekend while I was out with a friend. Well, I ended up leaving with the dealer and went back to his house to smoke crack all night long. From the first hit I was hooked. I mean this stuff was beyond just snorting cocaine.

It was fun at first but after a while I lost my job and ended up homeless and penniless. I decided that it was time to get my destructive life in order. I was in a really bad place. I turned myself into an alcohol recovery program at a hospital downtown. I can remember being angry, thin, shaking, and fearful because I was going through heavy withdrawals. I stayed there for a few months. I didn't have anywhere to go.

I was fed up and confused. The recovery team prescribed me a pill that would help me in my dealings with alcohol. It was called Antabuse and they said that I would get deathly ill if I tried to drink while I was on it. It helped me stay straight for a very long time.

I began seeing a therapist once a week. I was so angry that I blamed all my problems on my parents and my abusive home life. They had laid a very bad foundation for me. But I didn't realize that I had made terrible choices too and I was paying dearly for it. My life was one big mess. I didn't benefit much from the therapy. I was too wounded and blind to see the truth.

I don't know how I made it through life up to this point. It is only by the grace of God that I can even write this book. God commanded me to write it and He was very clear about it. He even told me when it needed to be completed. I was to get the book done in six months. We all have stories and God wants to use those stories to help others. I hope that my story will bring hope and healing to you. You are reading this book because it was ordained by God. I am consumed with tears just writing it because I thought I was doomed all my life. I went from one horrible mess to another, not knowing what to do. I strongly believe God is healing me even as I write these words on the pages. I wish I could go back in time and make things right. I wish I had the power to do that. But because of Jesus, all of the horrible things that have happened to us can be removed and we can be given a clean slate. All these generational iniquities can be washed away and he will give us another chance at life to do something amazing for the kingdom.

  I realize that it's hard to help someone else if you haven't been there or lived in their shoes. I've been an alcoholic, drug addict, involved with the occult, homeless, beaten, and abused. I was told as a young child that I would never amount to anything. I was tossed away like a piece of garbage. That was my beginning. The only thing that I found that brought me hope was Jesus Christ. He is my Lord and Savior. He is your only hope in this hopeless world. You are not alone, my friend. I don't know how a person can go through all these things and still be here and in their right mind. I personally have done so many drugs that my brain should be fried. But I completed my master's degree in 2010. Just imagine that. God healed my brain and if He can do that for me, He can do that for you.

I recently began sharing my story with a few people. When I tell them what I have been through they just look at me in shock. It was very hard for me to talk about my past. I actually just opened up this year and told my husband. Throughout our twenty years of marriage, my husband didn't have a clue what had happened to me in my past. I didn't think that people would accept me if I told them what I have done and what I have been through. Some of my family members don't even know what I have been through. If you met me you wouldn't think anything. I don't look like I went through any of those things. It's only by God's abundant mercy, healing, restoration power, and His grace that I am alive!

I believe the Lord seeks out hurting people to display His strong and mighty power. I would not have made it without Him. That is why I want to tell my story and take it everywhere—so I can give Him all the glory, praise, and honor that He deserves for what He has done for me! I know that it will be a blessing to people who have experienced the same things that I have endured in my life or are going through them right now. There's help and there's hope. God loves us so much and wants to restore all that is broken in our lives. He wants to give us back everything that the enemy has stolen from us.

God knows all about your hurt, pain, and sorrow. He saw your first tear. He knew you when you were in your mother's womb. God will use all the horrible things that you have been through and make it your message of hope to someone else. I often listen to an inspirational female Christian teacher who has a very successful television program. I have heard of her overwhelming past life and her testimony of the abuse that she endured. I often wonder how she could be sexually abused by her father until she was eighteen years old and still in her right mind. She has an anointed ministry that is helping millions of people find hope and restoration through Jesus Christ. She helps young women who are victims of a sex trafficking find freedom and a new life. She is using what she endured in her childhood to transform lives. I think that is so amazing!

It's up to us to pick ourselves up, take responsibility and move forward and as Proverbs 3:13 says that we are to seek knowledge and understanding from God through His word. We have to persevere to make it to the top. If we make the effort, He will meet us right where we are. We must be diligent and take the steps because He will meet us because He is always faithful. There are promises from God that He wants to fulfill in our lives. But we must condition our hearts to receive them.

It is time for you to take back all that the enemy has stolen. This is real, folks. Satan wants us to stay in our pit because he knows that as long as we stay wounded in our souls, he has the legal right to operate in our lives because we are letting him do so. We need to get our souls healed. When God gave me this revelation, it made me so mad! I know I was saved but, I was still having an immense amount of problems in my life that were created from the trauma I endured. This created deep wounds in my soul. This takes time and much effort to get these things healed and rooted out of your soul. Remember it took a lifetime to get wounded.

Please do not make the mistake of doing nothing. Pick yourself up right now where you are and say "No more!" And ask God to show you what is keeping you from receiving all that He has for you. God showed me that the enemy was in the courts of heaven accusing me of all the things I had done. Remember, none of us are perfect. We have all sinned and made horrible mistakes. But whose voice are you going to keep listening to? Right now, you can make the decision to trust God and say *no more.* Call out to Him. Dear God: I need your help! You are no respecter of persons; what You have done for others, You will do for me as well. You are able to turn my circumstances around for good. Please help me get to a place of peace as You work on me and my problems. Amen.

God will meet you right where you are! God gave me a new life and I will fight the good fight of faith every step of the way. Satan will never steal from me again! I have a destiny to fulfill. There's no turning back for me. I have been redeemed by the blood of Jesus! God has given us tools to defeat the enemy and we need to use them. I will be sharing these things with you in my book so that you can get free. You see you can ask Jesus into your heart, and that is the first step. But you have to use the knowledge and wisdom that is in God's Word to get free. It takes perseverance. It has taken me a long time of doing the right things and seeking Him for answers in my life for me to make any progress. Many of us are getting the wrong results because we are going about it the wrong way. Many people blame God, the government, the president, for their problems. They don't know that we have an adversary that wants to destroy us. That's his ultimate plan, so he will keep you in difficult cycles and patterns, which keeps you looking at your circumstances. As long as you are looking in the natural you will feel hopeless and defeated. I cried out to God for two years before I saw any answers. During those years, I knew I couldn't give up! God revealed to me that he had heard my cries, but, he wanted to hear me repent. So, I had no other choice but to press in and keep on pressing in.

    The enemy was working overtime so that I would not receive my breakthrough. He was bringing accusations before the throne, but it was my own fault. We need to read God's Word and know the truth. I have been deceived many times in my life. I often went in a direction that got me tangled up with the enemy and his lies and deception.

Chapter Five
My Early Twenties

When I was twenty years old, all my relationships with men had been doomed from the beginning. I met my first drug dealing boyfriend at the restaurant bar that I was working at. He would come in every week and just sit there and drink all afternoon until he got up enough nerve to say something to me. After a while, we started talking more and one thing led to another. I ended up moving in with him.

Eventually I quit working at the bar and began working downtown at a hair salon, where I managed to stay employed for a few years. I loved doing hair and I was happy working. But, I still drank a lot of alcohol and did a lot of cocaine during this time. After a year or so, I began doing drug drop offs with my boyfriend. I wasn't afraid.

I'm sure the drugs had given me a sense of fearlessness. Thank God I never got caught and arrested for dealing drugs. I was with this guy for a few years, but it turned out to be a very abusive relationship.

Most of my friends at this time were gay men that worked with me at the hair salon. I frequented a lot of gay bars and drank and did cocaine with them. During this time, I met another man while working at this salon and had an affair with him. When my boyfriend got wind of it, he kicked me out—after giving me a big black eye. Apparently, it was okay for him to cheat on me, but when I did it to him he didn't like it.

My next relationship began with dating another drug dealer. I would see him off and on, but we never became overly serious. Although he wasn't abusive, he carried a gun with him and I almost got killed one night standing outside a bar with him. Someone drove by and began shooting at us. My boyfriend pushed me down to the ground and saved my life. I wasn't afraid. Praise God for sparing my life because I could have easily been killed. The relationship only lasted a little while.

My drinking got worse. I would go out to bars with friends and couldn't remember how I even got home. I would often find myself abandoned by my so called friends and with some very bad people the next morning. This was frightening because I could never remember how I got there, who these people were, and what had happened during the night. I would wake up alarmed, scared, and fearful wondering where my friends were. Later my friend explained to me, "If you saw yourself on video when you're drunk, you would never drink again!" People couldn't handle being around me because I was a very angry and it came out when I was intoxicated. So most of the time, when my friends and I were out partying and I had too much, they had no other choice but to leave me alone to fend for myself. Unfortunately, I didn't make good choices with the people I hung around with—ideally they would have tried to at least get me home safe. I could have lost my life many times. I believe in my heart that the almighty God has spared my life many times.

During those crazy years of consuming massive amounts of cocaine and alcohol, I managed to get pregnant four times before I was twenty-six years old. I am very sorry to say that I terminated those pregnancies because I was in no shape to take care of a child. I was not in my right mind and my body was so full of drugs and alcohol. I have repented and cried over and over again about what I did. It was very hard for me to confess these things because I was so ashamed of what I had done. But I didn't have any hope and I didn't care about my life. I felt I had no other choice. I have just recently opened up and told my siblings about what happened to me. It has taken everything inside of me to write this book because I have been ashamed of myself all of my life. Believe me; I have paid dearly for these sins. It doesn't go away—I have been tormented by negative thoughts about these things. I am not making excuses for myself. I wish I could go back in time and make everything right.

If God hadn't planted seeds in my life when I was a young child, I can truly say that I would not be here today to write about it. Little did my dad know that when he dropped us off at the church on Sundays to get rid of us, he was actually saving my life? At least he did that much for me. I was a victim of abuse but I sinned too. The foundation of generational iniquity was already laid out for me, and I just lived out what I saw. It's not until you get sick and tired of living a defeated life that you begin to seek answers on how to get out of this pit of destruction. It's hard because you don't know where to begin.

Years went by and it was around 1985 that I met a man and we eventually got married. I stopped drinking once I got married. I knew that I needed to make big changes in my life. I was pretty messed up from all the drugs and alcohol and heavily addicted, but somehow, I quit drinking. I did it! Within two years I had a daughter. My marital relationship was doomed from the beginning, but as soon as I got pregnant I knew I had to make some healthy lifestyle changes for my life.

When my daughter was born it was the happiest day of my life, but I suffered horribly from post-partum depression. It was a really scary experience. I began hearing voices and was tormented by a spirit of fear. I went to a doctor to get help and she prescribed an anti-depressant. But I couldn't take it. Instead, I went cold turkey. I would not advise anyone to do this. I could have done something very stupid.

I went back to church and rededicated my life back to the Lord. My cousin was attending a church in the city at the time and I met her there for one of their weekly night services. As I sat in the service all I could do was cry. I mean I cried and cried for hours and hours in her arms. That's all I could do! It was the Holy Spirit touching me.

From that point on, things began to go well. But my husband did not want me in the church. He would tell me they just wanted my money, but I knew we didn't have any money. He was just another controller and abuser. The marriage didn't last very long because I wasn't going to take the abuse anymore. I had had enough. I ended up divorcing him and taking my small child and began a new life on my own. I left him on Mother's Day and it was a huge turning point in my life.

I later found out that my husband had a very bad gambling addiction and would spend hours at the race track spending all of our money. He was with other women, too. I once found a receipt from a hotel stay that had fallen out of his jacket pocket while I was cleaning out the closet. He was cheating on me with other women. He denied it. But it didn't really matter anymore. I was done.

About a year or so after my divorce, I met a man in the church where I dedicated my life. It turned out to be a different face but the same thing over again. He was a controller and an abuser too. That was it. I made up my mind to stay by myself and let God do what He had to do in me.

Things don't go away because you're saved; you have to know that you are severely wounded in your soul. I was just sick and tired at that point. I had to learn to seek God and let Him direct my steps and do what He wanted to do in my life. I had no business getting involved with any person. I was deeply wounded in my soul. I shifted my focus to the fact that I needed to get a job and find a place to live. I was still working in a hair salon part-time. One of the girls at the salon found out about my situation and she offered me a room in her house while I got on my feet and then I began searching for a full-time job.

I want to back track now. Even though my father was always accusing my mother of cheating on him, he was really the one that was cheating. He eventually booted my mother out of the house with no job and nowhere to go. My mother really didn't have any skills or know how to survive. She never even learned how to drive. But that's what abusers do, they keep you dumb and isolated from your family, friends, and things that may help you escape the madness of their control. And when he was finished abusing my mother, he threw her away. She later died of cancer when I was twenty-four years old.

After many years, I was finally able to confront my father. He was home alone one weekend and I went over to his house and began banging on the door. At this point in my life I was full of rage and anger. I needed to set things straight with him and get some things off my chest. I had been holding on to so much hatred and bitterness for so long. So I cornered my father and just exploded on him. He wasn't ready for it. But, I had to do it. He sat there and just listened to me scream like a crazy person. He knew I was serious. I told him that I wanted him to say he was sorry for everything that he had ever done to me as a child in word, deed, and action. I told him how he had ruined my life. I told him everything that I needed to say. After it all spewed out of my mouth, he just looked at me like he didn't know what happened. I was afraid that he wouldn't think he had done anything wrong. But he cried and said he was sorry. I believe he was. At that point I knew that I had made some progress in my life. It was at the very least a start in the right direction. It took me a long time to get all that anger out of me. God healed me little by little and he still is healing me today.

    Sometimes, as a way of releasing my anger or whatever you want to call it, I would spend time alone beating my pillow until I collapsed from using all my strength. But it felt good and I needed to get all that rage out of me. This went on for months and months. The rage consumed every part of me. Over time it lessened, but there was still a lot of stuff in me. I was in bondage over what I had committed in my life as well as what sins my ancestors committed. It doesn't go away. If you don't know what's there it's hard to understand. Our soul has layers upon layers of wounds from our sins and trauma and our family bloodlines that we are going to have to deal with. If our families haven't repented for their sins, then we are going to have to deal with the mess or our children will. I was stuck dealing with a whole lot of their messes on top of my own.

    Confronting my father was the best thing that I could have done for my life. I was so proud that I did it! I stood up to him and I forgave him. Then things began to change for me. I was able to begin to have a relationship with my father. The wounds were still present so it was a long healing process for me. During my relationship with my father I learned that many things about his childhood were just like mine—horrible. As an adult, my father found solace in his work. While he was working he was able to detach himself from his past. He became a workaholic and then came home and vented on all of us. It was when he wasn't working that he made everyone else's life a living hell.

My father ended up sharing with me many insights about his life and what he endured and how he was beaten and mistreated as a little boy. It was passed down to him and he passed it down to his children, which is a horrible way to live your life.

I managed to have a decent relationship with my father over time and I received help from him when I needed it. He went on to marry another woman and they had a couple of children. His behavior wasn't as bad and he even began going to church. But he still had the old character bents. He would often backslide and get involved in the occult. My dad's life would go up and down. He would be okay for a while and then he would revert back to his old behavior. My father eventually died of Alzheimer's. I was there at his bedside when he took his last breath. Sometimes when I look back and think about it, I believe he most likely wanted to forget about his past.

Do you see how these things get passed down from generation to generation? We don't have to buy into it. We have been bought by the blood of Jesus and we are new creations in Christ. You can trade in your parent's identity for a new one. It's not too late! It's never too late to change your life.

Chapter Six

Deceived by the Enemy

When you have wounds in your soul and want relief, you will do many things because you think you don't have choices. I once read a book entitled *Sanctuary*, which was about a man who created a healing process technique called "Energetic Balancing." I took a chance and tried it for about three years. I had a mentor when I first went on the program. She was a wonderful lady, but really wasn't able to give me the answers I needed.

Little did I know that this was a trap set up for me by the enemy? It was the occult disguised as something sweet and gentle. It was advertised as the church of healing so I bought into it. Things were going well until I started having unusual things happen to me. People began verbally lashing out at me on my job for no reason. I left that job for the sake of my peace and the attacks began again at my new job. I didn't know what was happening. Much later, I realized that I had opened the door to the occult and was I getting demonically attacked.

The church of healing could not explain why this was happening. After much prayer I received a revelation from God about my situation. He revealed to me that I was trying to serve two masters. I had one foot in Satan's camp and one foot in the Lord's camp. I don't know how I emotionally and spiritually survived this. I had made a contract with this church—a written agreement with my signature on it and I was giving money to this occult. I was putting money on an altar I wasn't aware of and ended up in a spiritual mess. We have to be careful folks.

I found out through revelation from God that I had made an agreement and signed a document with the devil. To make matters worse, I paid for the healing process every month. I was putting money on an altar so a curse came on me. I had to close the door that I had opened in ignorance.

The only way to find out if you are under a curse is for God to show you. Then you can deal with these things in the courtroom of heaven. You have to answer the accusations that the enemy is bringing against you. You really have no way of knowing these things except by revelation or repeated patterns and cycles. So you have to be very observant. Remember the enemy comes to kill, steal, and destroy. If you keep seeing the same things happening over and over again, most likely you are under a curse.

I have recommended some books to read at the end of this book that will open your eyes to the truth. I would suggest that you read them. You might as well repent of every last thing in your family generational bloodline. As I delved into teachings about generational curses, I was amazed at what I learned. Our ancestors did horrific things to survive. They were idolaters; they hunted and killed people, took land and possessions, sacrificed their children, participated in cannibalism, sold body parts, sold their children into sex slavery, and watched people get killed for amusement. Our adversary, Satan, keeps record of everything that you and your ancestors have done. Remember he is the accuser of the brethren.

Satan will find something in your past or your family generational bloodline to accuse you of so that you do not receive all the promises that

He has for you. But repenting is only one thing that you must do. After you repent you must cover that sin with the blood of Jesus and then release the Dunamis power from your spirit into your wounded soul so that every wound can be healed by the glory and the light of Jesus!

Like I stated before, as I began to break the curses in my life, things began to change, but it didn't happen overnight. Thankfully, my life has never been the same. I am still learning every day and I make it a point to read the Word and read books on these subjects. I also listen to different teachings on these subjects. I want to be able to reach out and touch people that are going through the same things. If you are experiencing these things, don't think you are losing your mind. Because these attacks are real and they are operating in many people's lives right in your church. I often hear things from people that are attending different churches who are facing the same sort of things that I experienced. And if we don't search out the truth and ask for God's revelations, we will remain stuck. I don't want anyone to remain stuck because you can't imagine what God has for you. I didn't realize the gifts and talents that were in me. I currently work in a new career that I never thought I could do. God took me from the pit to the palace and He can do the same for you!

Chapter Seven
Moving Forward

The individual that my father married happened to work for a Chicago public schools and she was able to put in a good word for me. I got a job in the school working as a teacher's assistant. Later, I decided to go back to college and earn a bachelor's degree while I raised my daughter.

I finally returned to church and God was beginning to show me things. I was involved in the music ministry and things were going well. God was working in my life and I was finally making some progress. I am not going to say that everything was perfect, because it wasn't! It's very hard trying to make a living as a single mother while going to school and making sure that your child is safe. I tried very hard to keep it all together.

It took me six long years to complete my bachelor's degree and to move on to a new career, but I completed it and graduated! Praise God!

After I received my degree, I got a job in the social work field. It was a good match for me and I excelled in it. My first job was working with children that had disabilities. It was a good place for me to begin. I had a lot of compassion for these children and their families. I, too, was just like them at one time. I didn't have a physical disability, but I couldn't learn in school. God healed my brain supernaturally and began to work in my life, but it was a still a struggle for me. I was never bright. I couldn't stand in front of people because I was afraid of failing and being ridiculed just like when I was a kid. Those tapes keep on playing in your mind until one day God comes in and says, "No more. You will not torment My beloved anymore."

Let me back track again. My father was a very strong person but also very naïve. He met a witch through one of his business partners and then got involved with Santeria, a type of witchcraft. I can remember going to one of the meetings with my father. I was curious about what he was doing. The witch put a curse on me and from that day I was tormented. I had anxiety and heard voices. I was vexed and I couldn't stand to be alone.

When people feel powerless, they resort to doing desperate things. My father went to these meetings so that he could learn to do things to people that he didn't like. I am speaking about these things because they can be passed down in families to the children and can be the cause of mental illness and other horrible things. When the door is opened to evil spirits a heavy price has to be paid. The only way to get free is to surrender your life to Christ so He can help you get free, although it may take some time.

The majority of people don't even know that strongholds are operating in their lives. We need to use all the tools that God gives us to get free. I speak in my heavenly language called tongues every day during my prayer time. A lot of believers don't believe in it, but this is one of the greatest tools that God has bestowed upon us as believers in Christ. God began giving me revelations about my life as I cried out to Him for two years straight. I cried out for two hours every morning and asked Him why my life was a mess. After two years, He began showing me by revelation what to do, and He gave me the steps. I had to follow through on the steps to get free.

My horrible life was caused by many generational curses operating in my life and my own iniquity. That meant that my life was going nowhere. I got ahold of a teaching by a wonderful man of God that was very helpful. He stated that if you have anything in your life where the enemy had a legal right, such as a generational curse you are stuck. God cannot go back on His word. He is bound by it. So you will stay in the same cycle until God reveals to you through revelation and the steps you must follow to get free. So many of us Christians are walking around with generational curses and we don't even know it!

I didn't know why things were happening to me in my life until I began crying out to God for those two years. I am writing this book to help people get free from the bondages and the chains of abuse. There are always a whole lot of other things that go along with bondage. Use your heavenly language people. You're talking directly to God! The devil does not know what you are talking about. Plus, it strengthens your spirit and gives you power over the enemy. Now, who doesn't want that? Amen!

My real freedom didn't manifest until forty years later. That's right! I was bound for forty years, and I don't want to go back. Now I am not going to say that I haven't stumbled, because I have. I have paid dearly for my mistakes, and that's why I am detailing this in my book. I want to use the time that God has given me to help others. I want to tell as many people as I can that there is freedom from generational curses and strongholds in your life. But you are going to have to want it with all of your heart and soul.

Let me talk about the soul. I believe that's where all our problems exist. We are given a new spirit once we get saved, so our spirit is saved and

God forgives our sins. But all those things that have been passed down to us, or trauma that has affected us, are hidden deep inside our soul. Those are the things that are affecting your life right now. The mental illness, the sickness, the lack, the family and marital problems are all coming from unresolved issues in your soul. So if you keep seeing a repeat of things showing up, or if you keep struggling in an area or many areas, most likely that's where it is coming from.

A wounded soul takes many years to heal. It is a work in progress. Many of us don't even know where to begin. You begin on your knees, asking God to reveal things to you that need to be dealt with. There are wounds in your soul and many of them are from our ancestors all the way back to the garden. That's where it all began. We have been cursed ever since Adam and Eve.

You will have to do the work to get free. But, praise be to God, there are answers and freedom from all these things. We are not supposed to be sick, oppressed, and broke. You are to be the head and not the tail. You should be happy and successful at your job! You should be lending and not borrowing. You should be living in houses you did not build. If you don't get healed from wounds in your soul, you will find yourself in the same old mess.

When I began receiving revelations from the Lord and had major breakthroughs in my life, I wanted more of it! But, it comes with a price. You are going to have to do it by putting God first in every area of your life and spending a good amount of time every day focused on Him and in His presence. Then He will show you what's behind your marital problems, sickness, and financial issues, and so on. These are long term generational iniquities that we are dealing with, folks.

We need to wake up and get busy kicking the devil out of our lives, taking territory back, and living the life that God promises for all of us that are born again. It doesn't mean that you won't have problems. But you will begin to see God's blessings being poured out and His favor, healing, and prosperity in your life.

The first major breakthrough that I received took me many months of breaking generational curses. I went through them over and over. Then suddenly I had a divine encounter with an angel. It made its presence known while I was at work. I can remember sitting at my computer one day, feeling down and discouraged. Out of the blue, an angelic being came into my office, put its hand on my shoulder, and kissed me on my cheek. I began to weep. I knew something big was coming—and it was.

Earlier that month I had sown a financial seed in a well-known Christian ministry. Shortly after, I got one of the biggest breakthroughs in my life. I was given a promotion at my job, and along with that came a huge raise. I was taken from the pit to the palace. I now use my God-given gift of writing to author books and I also use it in my job to do copywriting.

Previously, I had a lot of hatred for my father. He ruined my life, and those chains took a long time to heal. When curses have been spoken over you as a young child, those words do not go away. They begin to shape your life and you believe those lies until God shows you the truth of who you really are. God is the only One, my dear friends that can help you. There's nobody—no counselor, no hypnotist, no psychologist, no therapist, no life coach—that can set you free except Jesus Christ, our Lord and Savior! Believe me, I tried everything—New Age, energy healing, positive thinking, self-help books, and psychics. They're all lies of the enemy to keep you in bondage. You just keep on that same cycle until you get sick and tired of living in constant chaos.

When I finally had enough, I said loudly to God, "Lord what's wrong with me? Show me what's wrong. Why can't I get ahead? Why am I stuck? Why am I getting abused by people everywhere I go? Please help me! I don't know what else to do!"

Like I said previously, this went on for a couple of years until one day I was watching a very popular Christian television program. The guest was a preacher who was speaking about the courts of heaven and how he had been complaining about his son to his wife. He said that the Lord stopped answering his prayers. He kept praying and praying and one day he said to the Lord, "Why are You not answering my prayers?" He said the Lord told him to come to His courtroom. Yes, there's a real courtroom in heaven.

Now, because the man had spoken evil about his son, his son was in bondage. The son was depressed and couldn't get out of bed. The man had cursed his son, so to speak. He had to go before the court, repent, and ask Jesus to speak on his behalf and cover the sin with His blood, so that the son could be set free. You see, Satan had legal right to keep the man's son bound because he had opened the door for a curse to operate in his son's life. Once he broke the curse, repented, and covered it with the blood, his son was set free. Then Satan had no legal right to stay there. The son is now in full-time ministry and is a pastor.

You see, it's just like our wounds in our soul. When we have anger, bitterness, hatred, or unforgiveness about a person or situation and we have not repented or forgiven the person we are angry with, then Satan has legal right to set up camp and torment us, make us sick, steal from us, wreak havoc in every area of our lives. Wake up people! These are traps that the enemy has put in our paths to make us stumble. I fell for it every time and stayed stuck. This is some heavy stuff, but it can all be found in the Word of God. Most Christians are not aware that they are not receiving the promises of God. God wants to bless us more than we want to be blessed!

I want to talk about having a root of bitterness, because it is one of the most dangerous things that the enemy uses against believers. Once we get angry with a person or situation, the enemy is able to take root in our souls and cause a lot of distress in our lives. This happened to me. I began to have constant sickness in my body showing up like major infections, rashes, and diseases. Do you have an incident or person that you keep replaying in your mind? Well that's one of the signs. There are answers for you and it's all found in the Word of God. I got involved with a situation and made a judgement against someone and began to get sick. But, God is so good because His grace covers our mistakes. I got healed of bitterness and through that mistake I began studying the Word of God and teachings about bitterness.

Bitterness was a trap set up for me to steal my blessing. Once you let the enemy in, things will begin to happen and you will start to see major things like your car breaking down or a sickness that costs you thousands of dollars to get rid of. I had a reoccurring pain in my hip that did not go away for months. I couldn't sleep. But God revealed it to me in a dream that I was sitting on bitterness. So every time I sat down I would have this horrible pain in my hip.

One night, during this time of experiencing pain in my hip, I had a dream that the chair I normally sit in while I do my worship every morning had coffee grounds all over it. I looked up the meaning of coffee grounds and found it means bitter water. So I began doing work on the bitterness in my soul. I obtained freedom after I followed the steps that God had laid out for me. So when you think that it is okay to get mad at someone and give them a piece of your mind, you had better think twice about it. Ask the Holy Spirit to give you strength in this area. Don't fall for the trap; bitterness ruins relationships, marriages, businesses, churches, ministries and so on. Get healed my brothers and my sisters. Get wisdom in this because we all know that we have been in these types of situations.

I made a judgement about someone and even talked about them behind their back, which gave the enemy a legal right to torment me. Get healed in your soul and difficult people and situations will no longer affect you. I used to let myself get affected by everything because I was bitter and I would respond to situations bitterly. But, we as Christians cannot do these things anymore. That's why God's Word says to get wisdom and get understanding. I hope that these words of inspiration are helping you. Believe me, it has been one long journey for me and I am not going back to my old life. I want all that God has for me!

Chapter Eight
My Revelation

When God gives you a revelation it is one of the most powerful things that you could ever experience as a believer. I mentioned previously, that after crying out to Him for those two years, God finally answered me through a revelation that I received. It brought me clarity and freedom to act on it and begin my healing process. I mentioned that I began listening to this powerful teaching on the courts of heaven, then reading the accompanying book. Once I completed that teaching and mediated on it, I was ready to move onto the next step. I mentioned that I purchased another book that taught me how to break all the generational curses that were operating in my life. I didn't understand it all at the time, but I knew I had to do it to move on with it.

My Revelation

God was teaching me through revelation, how to get free so that I could help other people get free. This process took me many months to complete. The book took about two hours to read out loud. Yes, it was a very long process. Each time I read the book and broke the curses I felt a little weak for a few days. I contacted the distributor of the book and she told me that I had to do it until I didn't have any more symptoms. She stated that the reason I was not feeling well was that I was taking territory back from the enemy that had been stolen from my life. Like I said, I read that book over and over and over again until I was able to get free.

I can only imagine what my generational family has done in the past. I was in bondage from their sins that were passed down from my family and from my own sin. You have to remember we are going all the way back to Adam. It's frightening to think that our families killed other people for their land. They sacrificed their children to Baal. They sold their children and did all kinds of evil things to get ahead back then. People are still doing these things today. They are selling their children for a few dollars so they can eat. They are selling body parts in different countries. It is horrible; the things that people have done and are still doing today. I recently read a story in a *National Geographic* issue from April, 2011 about how one hundred and forty children were sacrificed in Peru over five hundred years ago. They found their bones on top of a mountain, and even found their little foot prints. These children, aged anywhere from five to fourteen, had to march to the top of the mountain to their deaths. The hearts of these individuals were removed. It's barbaric what people have done to secure land and possessions. I know that is hard to comprehend, but it is true. And these things are passed down to us.

Early civilizations were not following God. They were following the sun, moon, weather, and whatever they conjured up to worship. But to kill your child due to a bad storm is beyond my understanding. I wonder if these children knew what was going to happen to them. I can't imagine these horrible things. But nevertheless, these things happened and someone has to repent for these sins or they are passed down to us to deal with.

When I received revelation about why my life was such a mess I couldn't understand how I had to pay for something that someone did five hundred years ago. When I began breaking generational curses in my life, I was so eager to get free and there was no stopping me! But remember these things take time. As soon as I began breaking curses, the fact that I was sick for a while was evidence to me that something was there. I kept going until I did not feel anything anymore.

When I finally completed this process, my life began to explode wide open. It was as though something thrust me forward. I immediately got promoted at my job. I began to see favor in my life with people. All I can say is that God took me from the pit and to the palace. People around me could not believe what happened. But I knew what had happened was that the enemy had to take his hands off of my life. He could no longer torment me. He could no longer steal from me. I was no longer afraid.

Now I am doing things that I never even thought I could do. I still work in the social service field but I work in a much different capacity. I am so grateful for those two years of crying out! I got God's attention! He knew I meant business and I wasn't giving up! That is the key—to never, ever give up! Don't worry, in due time you will reap a harvest if you do not faint.

Now God is doing new things in my life. I committed to spending time with Him every day. I made the decision that I will not live without God's best in my life. I am never going back to that old miserable life. I have been made brand new and now I want to help others get free.

There are so many Christians sitting in churches that are not being fed what they need to hear. They are not moving ahead and that's why they are falling away. Nobody is teaching them how to get free. It's one thing to talk about it, but you have to give people principles to follow. Without them, they will stay in bondage. People stay unhappy, sick, depressed, and lonely. It breaks my heart. That's why I want to take my story to the masses and help others get free.

I have to take my message of hope to the lost and the hurting. Yes, we are saved. But, there are so many more nuggets of truth that God wants you to know. He loves us and wants us to be free in every area of our lives. We don't look good to the outside world if we are unhappy, sick, broken, complaining Christians walking around. It doesn't testify to God's greatness. Today people come up to me and ask me why am I so happy, and some have told me I am the nicest person they have ever met. Well, it's because I am happy. I am free!

Please take a look at the recommendations that I have included at the end of my book they will be a blessing to you. So you don't want to miss out on these anointed teachers. It's going to take time, so you have to be patient. Even though you go through this process you still may have other things that may creep up later. I read about a very prominent preacher who was in the process of building another church and all his money was stolen from him. After being completely financially wiped out, the Lord revealed to him that there was a generational curse that was operating in his life that he was not aware of. So the devil had legal right to go before the throne of God and accuse him of this. Now, I know you are saying really? How can this be?

God cannot go back on His word. So if your prayers are not being answered or you have found yourself stuck in the same mess over and over again, there's a good chance you that you are being accused by the accuser. It's up to you to go before the throne of grace and answer those accusations, repent of all of it, and cover them with the blood of Jesus. It's that easy! It made me so mad when I found out how easy it was. I

My Revelation

thought I had to fight the devil. No, the battle is the Lord's. We just have to diligently search for wisdom and learn to use the tools that God has given us. We must take back everything that the enemy has stolen from us and our families, beloved.

Praise God that there is so much great material out there about operating in the courts of heaven and soul healing. You are going to have to rise up from your place of discouragement and say, No more! You only have one shot in this world to make a difference. Remember nobody or nothing can keep you from your inheritance but you! Let God the Father, through the Holy Spirit; guide you into the most incredible life that you could ever imagine. Don't you want that? I want that for you, friend. Please, won't you take this time to pray this prayer with me? Heavenly Father, please show me the steps that I need to

My Revelation

get free. I don't know what's being held against me in the spirit realm but You do. Help me by Your Spirit reveal these things to me by revelation so that I can fulfill my destiny and purpose. Amen!

Chapter Nine
A New Life

When I finally became free I wanted to begin using my gifts and talents to advance the kingdom of God. I began with getting involved in raising money for my church. I was on a team of about seven people and within six months we raised one million dollars. After a few months God opened up the windows of heaven and blessed me with an incredible job of raising money for the non-profit that I now work for. I was immediately promoted with a very large increase. I began writing for the company that I work for. I am now writing all of the appeal letters. I have already completed my first book *The Divine Appointment*, and what you are reading is my second book. I did not know that I had these gifts inside of me.

A New Life

In 1994, I met a man while working at the school I mentioned earlier and we began dating. He had three children from his first marriage and he had sole custody of them. I had one daughter from my first marriage. He was and is a very nice man. He was the kind of man that I had been searching for all my life. In 1997, we got married in court and then got officially married in church a little later. All of our children were going to church and serving in the church.

Things were going well, but nothing is ever perfect. He is a great role model to the children. But problems existed because we had children from two different marriages and these children were wounded. We had to work really hard to keep everyone happy. Plus, I still had issues and so did he. We both came from bad marriages, so it has taken the good Lord to do a lot of healing in both of our lives.

A New Life

I have been married now for twenty-three years. There have still been challenges, but it has been the best relationship that I have ever entered into. My husband and I both serve God the best we can. We are pretty busy at our church. It is a small church in our community, but we are both grounded there. I think that is important. We need to get grounded somewhere so God can do the work in our lives. We have to be consistent and lay down whatever junk we have at the cross and let Him take care of it.

Like I have stated before, when we get saved, our spirits are made new, but we have lots of junk. Earlier I spoke about how God revealed to me through a dream that I had a root of bitterness operating in my life it was an ancient root from my generational bloodline. Then things began showing up in my life and I was struck by confusion. I began to get sick in my body, which resulted in money spent on doctors, hospital bills, and medications. I also had on going issues with my car breaking down. I previously mentioned that I had this dream that I was sitting on coffee grounds, then after looking it up in the Christian dictionary to find out what it meant, it revealed it was bitter water. This was God's way of revealing to me that I was sitting on a root of bitterness. And that is why I began to have a myriad of things show up in my life.

It's not necessarily God trying to teach you a lesson. It could be because the enemy has gained access and has legal right to torment you either by your own sin or the sins of your generational ancestors. These things take time. Remember, if your ancestors sinned, you will be affected by their iniquity. You may even have character bents that make you lean towards a certain behavior or weakness, and so one way to spot a root of

A New Life

bitterness is how you react to certain situations that come up in your life. Are you prone to get upset, angry, and take revenge and make the person pay for what they did to you? The Word of God tells us in the book of Leviticus, Chapter 19, that we should not seek revenge or bear a grudge against anyone. Vengeance is mine says the Lord!

Chapter Ten
Generational Curses

Many people in the church today do not know anything about these generational curses. I learned that this truth is real and it is playing out in many believers' lives today. We have to wake up and know that sin is sin and it brings many consequences and blocks the blessings of God. If it is not repented of, it is most likely playing out as a curse or stronghold.

I had been saved for many years, but I was stuck. I couldn't move ahead. I was always being confronted with some circumstance and I thought it was everybody else. Why were they getting the promotion or the raise? Why couldn't I get ahead?

It didn't matter how hard I tried, I was stuck! Why would a loving God keep me stuck? After all, His word says in Jeremiah 29:11, *I know the thoughts and plans that I have for you, says the Lord. Thoughts and plans for welfare and peace and not evil, to give you a hope in your final outcome.*

Well I wasn't seeing His good plan playing out in my life. But, I previously mentioned that God showed me, after those two years of crying out to Him, just what my problem was. I was being held back because of these things. Oh, I had my own sin, but there was something else that the enemy was holding against me. Therefore, I was not receiving all of God's promises and blessings in my life.

Like I said previously, I was watching a very popular Christian show one evening. I was feeling down but still searching for answers. There was a man of God preaching about the courts of heaven.

I froze and listened to what he was saying. That's it! It was God speaking directly to me. After two years of crying out every morning for two hours—finally my revelation had finally arrived. But like I mentioned before it was going to take work on my part. You see, God gives you the revelation but you're going to have to work it out. You have to follow the steps that He gives you.

So I got my revelation from God, then I bought the CD and book and begin to saturate myself in it. My next step was to purchase a book on repentance that was recommended. This amazing book opened my eyes to the power of repentance. I began repenting for everything in my family's generational bloodline. I would read the prayers out loud. It took me two hours to speak all the prayers out loud, and the next day I would be sick. Remember, the author of the book had stated that you would feel physically sick in your body because of the sin. I did feel pain and illness.

When I called the distributor of the book and asked her how many times I was to pray these prayers, she said as long as it takes and that I would know.

So I prayed those prayers consistently for many months. Then things began to happen. I felt this overwhelming supernatural power come over me! It was like I had super powers! Then one night God gave me a powerful dream. I was running up the stairs in a building. All of a sudden, I saw the glass from a very large window explode. A dolphin had flown through the window right in front of me. It was like God saying, "It's your breakthrough!" And it was my breakthrough!

During that time, I was volunteering at my job with a fundraiser. Previously I mentioned that I had assisted in a church fundraiser so I learned how to ask people for money "cold calling" over the phone. I had the technique pretty well down pat. Well during the fundraiser, I raised the most money, and it opened a door for me. In addition to the phone calls, I had to write all the fundraising letters and so I submitted a sample. I had become a pretty good writer in college.

God was getting ready to move in my life and of course the enemy was going to put up a fight, which, he did. Now I need to backtrack to before all of the fundraising opportunity had happened. Remember that I had mentioned that I was sitting in my office one day, feeling very depressed. And that angel came into my office, I will never forget this! He was most likely so happy for me to finally do something for me! But, I didn't know that his presence is what put everything into motion and what helped everything fall into place. Praise God! Praise God!

Oh, praise God for all the great things He had done! This event catapulted my life to a whole new level.

It's time to take back everything that the enemy has stolen from us—our marriages, families, and our future. We are all here to make a difference in the world. God has had a plan for your life since before you were born. But we have to do the work and seek knowledge, wisdom, and understanding and rise up and take a stand.

There is no reason for you to be broken, depressed, and full of anger about your situation. There are key steps that you must follow and begin your journey of breaking the bondages in your life. You not only want to read the Word each day but you also need to search out available materials that teach about these things. I love books and when I find one that really resonates with my soul I will often sit and read it in a day.

When you are hungry you will do anything to get free. So, my friend, rise up, pick up your mat, and walk into a new life of freedom. No more being depressed about your situation.

    I don't know what made me cry out for those two years. I don't know where I found the strength even in my depressed state to get up every morning and keep on pressing in. All I can say is that God heard my cry! I don't understand why it took so long—it puzzles me to this day. But I think it's because there was so much demonic influence in my life trying to block my breakthrough.

    Remember to get your hands on the books that I have recommended. It's no accident that you are reading this book today. God led you to read my book and planted the seeds to begin the healing process in your life. Now you must move forward and take back what is yours! Please do not live another moment without receiving what is rightfully yours, what God has already promised to you from the beginning.

I know that as you are reading this, you are probably thinking how this happen for me! I know I was so down and discourage too. But now you can take this information and begin getting down to business. This is your first big step toward freedom. It is going to take time and patience to get free. Be sure to give yourself the time that you need. It's not going to happen overnight. You have to persevere! You have to be determined that you will not live without what is yours! Continually ask for wisdom, knowledge, and revelation. You have to go after it. Going to church on Sunday morning is great, but the real victory comes from seeking Him consistently every day and putting Him first. This is not a game. This is survival people. We have a real enemy who would like nothing more than to take us out. Now you can clearly see from my story that Satan had a plan to destroy my life. He was already attacking me at the age of three while I slept by sending a demon to attack me. Because he knew that God was going to use me. So he has tried very hard to put up roadblocks and steal all my blessings. It's only by God's grace that I am here. Praise God that he never let me go!

Recommended Reading

Operating in the Courts of Heaven, 2014
Book and CD
By Robert Henderson
Robert Henderson Ministries
www.RobertHenderson.org

Repentance, 2009
Cleansing your generational bloodline
Book
Restoring the first estate
By Natasha Grbich

Healing the wounded Soul, 2017
Book
By Katie Souza
www.expectedendministries.org

Soul Decrees, 2015
Book
By Katie Souza
Eleven Eleven Enterprises
Katie Souza Ministries

The Glory Light of Jesus Heals your Soul, 2011
Audio CD
By Katie Souza
www.expectedendministries.org

www.ingramcontent.com/pod-product-compliance
Lightning Source LLC
LaVergne TN
LVHW011721060526
838200LV00051B/2986